BUILD YOUR CLEAR VISION

A Creative and Strategic Workbook to
Clarify Your Purpose and Build What's Next
Using the C.L.E.A.R. Vision Framework

LISA GUILLOT

Copyright @2025 Lisa Guillot

All rights reserved.

BUILD YOUR CLEAR VISION

A Creative and Strategic Workbook to Clarify Your Purpose and Build What's Next Using the C.L.E.A.R. Vision Framework

ISBN: 978-1-83556-451-6 *Hardback*
978-1-83556-452-3 *eBook*
978-1-83556-453-0 *Paperback*

CONTENTS

Introduction   VII

1
Reclaiming Your Creative Power   12

2
Releasing Judgment   24

3
The C.L.E.A.R. Vision Framework:
Building and Embodying Your Clear Vision   30

4
Your Clear Vision Rising   87

Acknowledgments   90

About the Author   92

Spread the Word!   93

To my bright kids.
Love you.

INTRODUCTION

You're ready to build something that matters, something greater than yourself and uniquely yours. But right now, that vision feels a little fuzzy, buried under distractions, responsibilities, and endless "Could I?" questions. Friend, that's about to change.

Hi, I'm Lisa Guillot, author of the best-selling book *Find Your Clear Vision: A New Mindset to Create a Vibrant Personal or Professional Brand with Purpose*. This workbook is your hands-on companion, a revised and expanded deep dive into the C.L.E.A.R. Vision Framework that has helped hundreds of creatives, leaders, and visionary thinkers bring their ideas to life.

Inside, you'll find fresh questions, updated practices, and AI-powered tools to help you bring your vision to life with clarity and soul. You don't need to have read the original book to get started (though I highly recommend it; it's a great read). Everything you need is in your hands right now.

If you commit to this journey with me, here's what you can expect:

- Creative ideas that actually get somewhere
- Energetic rituals that expand your personal power
- Strategy that is both soulful and sharp to bring your Clear Vision to life

This workbook is where mindset, energy, creativity, and strategy come together, throw on some house music, and get to work.

You don't need to follow a strict timeline, but I'll offer you options. Some folks like to dip in and out as needed; others move through it like a course. Either way, the invitation remains the same: go as deep as you desire.

This workbook is for you if:

- You're a creative with a million ideas but no clear direction
- You're a leader or entrepreneur who knows you're meant for more but can't see the next step
- You're a coach or consultant with wisdom to share but feel stuck about how to shape it
- You're a purpose-driven human who wants to live and lead with meaning

This workbook may not be the right fit if:

- You want quick hacks, silver bullets, or plug-and-play success formulas
- You're not open to reflecting on your mindset, energy, or beliefs
- You'd rather play small than risk feeling silly or being seen

Picture yourself a few months from now. You've stopped spinning your wheels. You know what you're building. You're not just dreaming your Clear Vision; you're living it.

No, it's not magic. But it is powerful.

This work is grounded in reality, yet it's designed to help you build the next-level version of your life, your livelihood, and your self-expression.

You won't just think about your vision.
You'll embody it. Plan for it. Align with it.
And ultimately, build it with me as your visionary guide.

INTRODUCTION

Clear Vision Journey Tracker

You don't need to do this all at once, but you do need a way to see where you've been and where you're going. That's where your Clear Vision Journey Tracker comes in.

Think of this as your map, your mirror, and your reminder that progress is happening even when it feels slow. This will help you track your movement through the C.L.E.A.R. Vision Framework, reflect on your wins, and stay connected to your growth over time.

You can download a printable version of this tracker at:
www.bebrightlisa.com/books

Save it, print it, hang it near your desk, or tuck it into your journal.

How to Use It:

- Mark your start date. This isn't about hitting deadlines; it's about honoring the moment you said yes to yourself.
- Note when you complete each phase. C.L.E.A.R. isn't linear. You might revisit parts more than once, and that's perfect.
- Use the reflection prompts to capture insights. This is a living record of your evolution.
- Celebrate along the way. When you complete a section, reward yourself with something meaningful, big or small.

> **Bright Tip:**
> Invite a friend to go through this workbook with you. Some people treat it like a book club or sacred circle to stay accountable together. If you're part of one of my coaching programs, bring this tracker to our sessions. We'll use it to anchor your work and build momentum.

Awesome. You've now clarified how you'll move through the journey.

Now, it's time to look at where you're going.

The C.L.E.A.R. Vision Framework

A 5-part framework for turning ideas into reality

You're about to move through the five phases of the C.L.E.A.R. Vision Framework, a transformational process that blends creative exploration, energetic alignment, and grounded action. Use this page as a quick reference guide throughout your journey.

C: Clear Concept: Your Why

Discover your Clear Vision Concept with this foundational declaration:
"I am here to... and this is important because..."

This is the heart of your vision. You'll explore what truly matters, how you want to contribute, and the deeper purpose behind it. This is a time to dream, explore, and claim your purpose in the world.

L: Legit Vision: Quick Vision Check

Your Clear Vision must be legit and long-lasting.

Here, you'll confirm that this is the vision you're ready to commit to. Think of this as the moment you go from "maybe" to "I'm in."

E: Expanded Energy

Your energy is your greatest resource. This section is all about releasing what drains your energy, aligning your mind, body, and soul with chakra-balancing tools, and finding your Visionary Values to make aligned choices.

A: Aspirational Success

In this phase, you'll visualize success and translate it into actionable steps. You'll choose between a 90-day sprint or a 12-month vision track, then use AI tools to support and guide your implementation.

Structure doesn't kill creativity; it supports it.

INTRODUCTION

R: Rooted in Celebration

We use celebration as fuel to stay motivated and aligned because celebration is a strategy. In this phase, you'll learn to design your daily, weekly, and milestone celebrations.

Hard work is one tool; so are joy, rest, and fun. Use them all.

Now that we know where we're going, let's get started.

Chapter 1

RECLAIMING YOUR CREATIVE POWER

What is Creativity?

Creativity isn't a luxury reserved for artists with gallery shows, dancers on stage, or the effortlessly cool person with that freaking amazing wardrobe. Creativity is a way of being, a mindset that lets you approach life with curiosity, courage, and soul.

At its core, creativity is the art of becoming more of who you truly are. Not the buttoned-up, endlessly optimized version of yourself, but the raw, radiant, real you—the one who isn't afraid to try something new, take up space, and shine imperfectly and powerfully.

Creativity is the energy you bring into a room, the quirks and eccentricities that set you apart.

It's the secret tool that transforms good leaders into visionaries and successful careers into meaningful legacies. When you embrace a creative mindset, you open the door to discovering your Clear Vision.

But somewhere between board meetings, family responsibilities, and endless pings, your creative spark got muted.

Don't worry if you feel like you've lost your creative edge or never had it to begin with. I'll show you how to bring your creativity to life.

Why Creativity Matters

A creative mindset doesn't just make you feel more "inspired." It helps you lead. It allows you to see connections others miss. It fuels innovation, deepens relationships, and keeps you aligned with your bigger vision, even on the messy days.

This is your invitation to turn the volume back up on your creative voice.

You don't need to blow up your life or start wearing all black to call yourself creative. You just need to remember what it feels like to be deeply in tune with your instincts, intuition, and ideas—and to trust that your ideas matter.

The Creative Process: A Real-World Metaphor

When I was a teenager, I learned how to shape my creativity in a humid, damp basement in Mid-Missouri with a tiny woman named Naomi.

Imagine a small woodland gnome with wispy gray hair, brown corduroy pants, smudged glasses, and hands so strong they could mold mud into magic—that was Naomi.

She taught wheel-throwing classes out of her home, and it was there that I learned what it meant to create something from nothing. I became a potter.

The first step in throwing a pot is wedging a block of clay—a messy process of beating, folding, and pressing the clay to remove any air bubbles. Skip this part, and the air bubbles will explode in the kiln.

That stuck with me.

BUILD YOUR CLEAR VISION

Because that's what building a Clear Vision feels like, too.

You start with a messy lump of an idea. You work out the bubbles and fight the wobble. You learn when to press and when to let go. And slowly, something begins to take shape—not just a piece of art, but a future vision so big it creates change.

Creativity isn't magic. It's a practiced process. And it starts with a mess that needs molding.

The Six-Part Creative Process

Let's clarify how this process works. You'll return to this throughout the workbook.

1. **Release Judgment**

   I'll teach you how to let go of the belief that you're "not creative enough" or "it's too late to start." Releasing judgment opens space for insight.

2. **Brainstorm**

   You will generate fresh ideas without needing them to be perfect. Use visioning, wordplay, AI prompts, and creative exploration to uncover what's possible.

3. **Clarify Your Vision**

   You will choose the idea that matters most. Define it with language that feels alive, aligned, and true. This becomes the foundation of your Clear Vision.

4. **Laser Focus**

   You will decide how to show up for your vision and for how long by channeling your energy toward one idea and committing to a time frame that supports success.

5. **Create a Roadmap**

   You will build a strategy for bringing your vision to life. Break it down into milestones, timelines, rituals, and aligned support.

6. **Share It**

   Now, it's time to bring your vision into the world using your expertise, voice, brand, and platforms to share your message or make meaningful change with confidence.

Bright Tip:
Print or bookmark this page as a quick reference.

Bright Tool: Define Your Creative Identity

Creativity isn't just something you "do;" it's a way you move through the world. The Creative Identity exercise will help you rediscover your unique creative flavor: the activities, environments, and moments that bring you joy, freedom, and inspiration.

Use this time to brainstorm and play. Jot notes in the margins, doodle in the corners, or keep a special notebook just for this journey. I use an unlined journal with thick paper so the ink doesn't bleed through.

I carry the journal and the books I'm currently reading in a fabric bag, like the kind you'd take to the farmers market, so I can capture inspiration on the move, wherever I am.

There are no wrong answers here. We're just molding the block of clay with curiosity and discovery.

Timing

This step is foundational to your Clear Vision work. Give it space. I recommend spending a day or two exploring your Creative Identity and who you are before moving forward.

Revisit the practices often, especially when creating the **Pop & Drop Thinking** in the next chapter.

1. What sparks creativity, joy, and flow for me?

Make a list of at least 15 activities that give you life. These can be tiny moments, outrageous ideas, or simple pleasures.

I'll go first:

- Build a puzzle
- Design a dreamy tablescape for dinner with fascinating people
- Write a love note to my kids

- Write poetry
- Get dressed as an act of vibrant maximalism
- Brainstorm with a friend over strong coffee
- Eat anything with lemon
- Dance in the kitchen

2. In a world without limits, what would I try?

Push the boundaries of what feels possible. This is your permission slip to go wild, no editing allowed.

I'll go first:

- Scuba dive in the Red Sea
- Attend a silent rave
- Live in Costa Rica for a winter
- Spend six months alone writing in San Francisco
- Take a sabbatical to walk the Camino de Santiago
- Learn to fly on a trapeze

3. When do I feel most creatively alive?

Think about time, space, mood, and surroundings. Where are you? Who are you with (if anyone)? What's the vibe?

I'll go first:

- Early mornings before the house wakes up
- During my commute with no noise, just my thoughts
- On lazy Sunday mornings with my cat Sunday (yep, that's my cat's name)
- Mid-yoga flow, when my mind finally stops racing
- Right after watching Beyoncé do anything
- Having deep conversations with spiritual gurus in Santa Fe
- Talking strategy with like-minded entrepreneurs at Soho House in Chicago

4. What creative work have I already done?

List past experiences that required creativity, even if you didn't recognize them as such at the time. Parenting, launching a product, designing a website, writing copy, throwing a fabulous party, it all counts.

I'll go first:

- Designing the first Pottery Barn Kids website
- Writing my best-selling book
- Leading visioning sessions for senior execs
- Coaching creatives and CEOs through reinvention
- Becoming a professional Tarot reader
- Raising wildly creative and kind-hearted humans

Creative Reflection Prompt

Look over your answers and journal:

- What do these examples have in common? What am I doing?

- What themes or feelings show up again and again? Who am I being?

- What are the qualities of a person who has lived a life like this? What would people call someone like this?

Circle your favorite five words that describe the creative essence of this person.

Guess what? These five words are a mirror of who you are at your most creative.

Complete the sentence stem: "I am someone who loves…."

I'll go first:

I am someone who loves spirituality, deep conversation, brainstorming with friends, and writing in fun, funky urban spaces.

Now, you have a list of fun things to do when you want to reclaim and embody your creative identity.

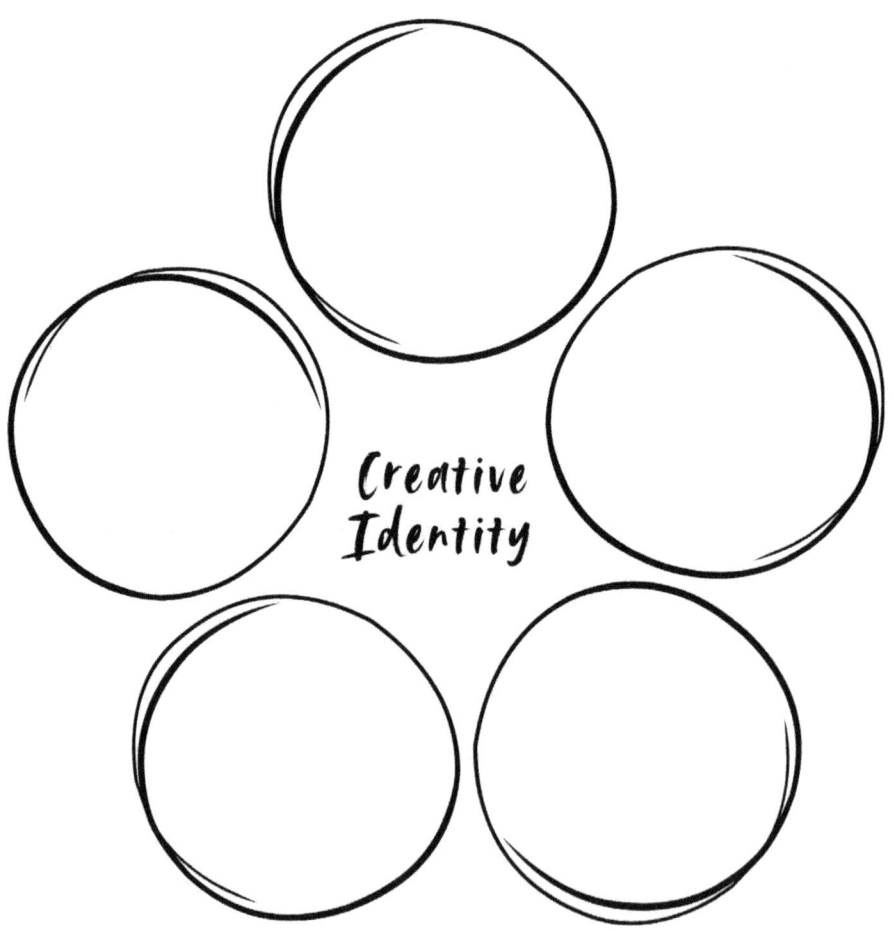

> **Bright Reminder**
> This isn't a one-and-done exercise; it's a living document. Keep adding to the list as you move through the workbook. Your creative identity will evolve alongside your Clear Vision. Let it grow.

Now that we've started to bring our creativity to the surface, let's weed out any remaining air bubbles standing between us and our vision.

Chapter 2

RELEASING JUDGMENT

Let's Get Out of the Drop

Let me state the obvious: you're here because your Clear Vision feels fuzzy. You're smack dab in the Messy Middle—that blurry space where answers feel elusive and overthinking becomes a full-time job. Trust me, I've been there. I've got a PhD in rumination and a master's in overanalyzing.

And if you're the type who's used to a color-coded calendar, an inbox at zero, and spreadsheets that would make a CFO weep, this lack of clarity can feel… unsettling. You're used to being the one with the answers. But when it comes to your next chapter, it's giving blank stare.

Good news: you're not alone.

Clients of mine, big-deal ones, the kinds with drool-worthy LinkedIn bios, have said things like:

"It sounds silly, but I don't know what I want to be when I grow up."

RELEASING JUDGMENT

Behind the job title is a very real desire to shift into something more meaningful and make real change, but judgment is in the way. That voice in your head gets louder:

- "You should have this figured out by now."
- "What's wrong with you?"
- "Maybe it's too late."

Let's shut that down.

This is the part where things get interesting. It's where space opens up for what's next, but only if you stop crowding it with shoulds, shame, and outdated beliefs.

So no, this isn't another self-improvement to-do, or a spiritual bypass. It's permission to get curious.

What if this fog you're in is actually the first sign of clarity trying to break through?

Fun, right?

Bright Tool: Pop and Drop Thinking

Pop and Drop Thinking is a tool I created to help you track your energy (which, bonus, will save you time). Because your Clear Vision needs time and energy to grow.

Pop Thoughts light you up. They sound like:

- "I wonder what would happen if I started a podcast? That sounds fun!"
- "Ooooh, what if I planned a sabbatical next summer to Greece?"
- "What if I totally disrupted the design world with this idea?"

Drop Thoughts are energy vampires. They sound like:

- "I've been doing this too long to change now."
- "I'd never make money doing that."
- "Who do I think I am?"

We need to bring awareness to both because you can't shift your mindset around what you don't see.

Your Assignment:

Grab a page (or two). Draw a line down the middle. Label one column **DROP** and the other **POP**.

RELEASING JUDGMENT

Drain the Drop:	**Amplify the Pop:**
On the Drop side, list everything that drains you: people, tasks, conversations, thoughts, responsibilities, and habits. Get it all out. Be ruthless.	Now, the fun part. On the Pop side, what gives you life? List the people, ideas, environments, food, movement, music, work, and actions that make you feel like *you*.

Think back to your Creative Identity words. That, plus this, is your Pop Zone.

Reflect:

- What's one Drop thought you could release, delegate, or reframe?

- What's one Pop activity you can schedule this week?

Write it down. Then go do it.

Yes, we're doing deep work, but that doesn't mean we can't make it fun.

So, delegate as many drops as you can and pop it like it's hot.

A client recently told me:

"I didn't realize how heavy I'd been feeling until I started naming my Drop thoughts. It was like I cleared space to actually want again. And I haven't wanted anything in a long time."

That's what the Creative Identity and Pop and Drop Thinking are about: making space for desire, possibility, and the parts of you that still know how to dream.

You Are Here → Foundation Phase: Complete!

You've just moved through the first two chapters.

You've dropped the old narratives. You've got your energy and creative mojo.

Now, we move to the C.L.E.A.R. Vision Framework: **The beginning of your new story.**

This journey will challenge you.

It's going to get messy because you don't know the answers yet, which is okay.

Before we dive in, repeat after me:

- I give myself permission not to know what this looks like yet.
- I give myself permission to be wildly unrealistic.

This is your sacred time.

We're not aiming for perfection; we're aiming for new possibilities.

Chapter 3:

THE C.L.E.A.R. VISION FRAMEWORK: BUILDING AND EMBODYING YOUR CLEAR VISION

Part 1: Your Clear Concept, Creativity Meets Clarity

Remember that feeling of possibility you had as a child—that pure, unfiltered excitement when an idea lit you up from the inside? Like discovering a new way to play pretend or a new song to sing?

That's what we're reclaiming today, only now, with your wisdom and experience.

Your Clear Vision is the disco ball (stick with me here) that reflects your brilliance in all directions, illuminating not just what you do but who you are at your core: who you connect with, where your light shines, and how it grows. (This is why I give away disco balls at my talks.)

THE C.L.E.A.R. VISION FRAMEWORK: BUILDING AND EMBODYING YOUR CLEAR VISION

It's time to step beyond the confines of "shoulds" and "busy" into a space of possibility.

A client recently said to me:
"Now that I practice staying in the Pop, I find so much joy in getting curious about what feels good to me. It's DELIGHTFUL to surprise myself. I feel like a little kid splashing in mud puddles on the way home from school."

Friend, this is a C-suite executive. Jumping in mud puddles.

This is the energy we're inviting in.

The C.L.E.A.R. Vision Framework

The C.L.E.A.R. Vision Framework is your roadmap for transformation, with each letter representing the next step:

- **C: Clear Concept**: What you're here to create
- **L: Legit & Long-Lasting**: Goals that align with your true self (and you won't get bored with in six months)
- **E: Expanded Energy**: The vitality to sustain your vision
- **A: Aspirational Success**: Your unique definition of what success means to you
- **R: Rooted in Celebration**: Honoring each step of your journey with a little fun

In this chapter, we begin with your **Clear Concept**, your North Star. But instead of a distant point of light, it's a declaration of who you are and what you're here to create.

Unlike the exhausting pursuit of purpose or the pressure to "follow your passion," your Clear Concept emerges from curiosity.

Build Your Clear Concept

This is where we pull all the pieces of the pie together—the inklings, the creative impulses, the Pop energy—and start shaping it into something you can actually name, own, and build from.

You don't need to know exactly where it's going yet. Just have the desire to begin.

Step 1: Define Your Clear Concept

(1-hour or over a week)

At the end of this step, you will have the foundational sentence stem:
"I am here to... and this is important because..."

This is your Clear Vision declaration. It helps your vision take shape outside your mind and into the world.

This is a time to explore and play—no censoring, no second-guessing. Remind yourself of your Creative Identity and let that persona lead the way as you brainstorm.

THE C.L.E.A.R. VISION FRAMEWORK: BUILDING AND EMBODYING YOUR CLEAR VISION

Bright Tool: Visioning Questions

Doodle, journal, or take voice notes—whatever way you like to brainstorm—just answer the questions with an open, non-judgmental mind.

- What conversations do I want to be a part of in the future? What energizes me?

- What conversations do I not want to be a part of? What drains me?

- What do I want to spend more time doing?

- What makes me feel alive?

THE C.L.E.A.R. VISION FRAMEWORK: BUILDING AND EMBODYING YOUR CLEAR VISION

- What do I believe in?

- What makes me different?

- What do people ask me for advice on?

- What is something I want to change in the world?

THE C.L.E.A.R. VISION FRAMEWORK: BUILDING AND EMBODYING YOUR CLEAR VISION

- What unique skill do I possess that others recognize in me?

- What do I want to be known for?

Now, take a break.

Go do something that puts you in the Pop: dance it out, walk it off, or simply close the workbook and let your brain refresh.

Step 2: Focus

I want you to look back at your answers and circle what lights you up or sounds exciting.
Cross out anything that feels like a "should" or an old story. Be brutal.

Clear out the junk so more light can come through.

Step 3: Expand

Now, take your favorite ideas that are still on the list from Step 2, and go big.

Ask:
"If there were no limits or barriers, what would I do now?"

If you removed all the barriers, all the "why not" and "who am I?" What would you do?

Continue to highlight recurring words, energy, or themes.

Write down new ideas. Go for at least three new ones.

Elaborate on your favorites.

This is where your north star starts to reveal itself.

Step 4: Repeat Step 2

Viciously cross out anything that's going to bore you in a month or doesn't light you up.

THE C.L.E.A.R. VISION FRAMEWORK: BUILDING AND EMBODYING YOUR CLEAR VISION

Now, look at your delightful, messy list and see if there's an idea that gives you butterflies—makes you feel warm inside or scares you just enough to give you the good kind of goosebumps.

That's your future energetic self sending a sign. Grab a bright highlighter and mark it.

Then, review your list and begin highlighting the concepts, thoughts, and ideas that feel full of possibility.

Step 5: Why is this Important?

Now, you have a refined list of ideas that you can see yourself creating and bringing to life.

Looking at what's left, ask yourself this question for each of the ideas that are left:

- Why is this important?

If nothing comes up, it's probably not that important to you.

I typically ask my clients this question 3-4 times narrow down the concept's importance to it's true why.

You must figure out why this idea or vision is important to you—because when it gets hard, when you lose sight of what matters most, when your friends try to talk you out of it, when you mess up or want to quit, you'll need to return to your why.

Knowing why your Clear Concept matters will keep you laser-focused and committed to creating it. Even when the outcome looks hazy or life gets in the way, your why becomes an inner mantra—one that keeps you motivated to design your Clear Vision every damn day.

Finally: Craft Your Declaration

Return to the sentence stem:
"I am here to..." (Choose a verb that activates you: create, lead, inspire, connect, build, etc.)

"...This is important because..." (Here's where your why lives.)

Examples for Inspiration:

I'll go first:
"I am here to guide others to find and build their Clear Vision. This is important because, for generations, creativity and leadership were reserved for a select few—but today, everyone deserves to share their vision and shape what comes next."

THE C.L.E.A.R. VISION FRAMEWORK: BUILDING AND EMBODYING YOUR CLEAR VISION

Stephanie:
"I am here to use my story to spark conversations about what true inclusion looks like. This is important because every voice deserves to be heard and every person deserves to belong."

Olivia:
"I am here to build my personal brand so I can inspire others to lead with authenticity and courage. This is important because when we show up as ourselves, we give others permission to do the same."

It's your turn. Write your Clear Vision Declaration.

Print it. Tape it on your mirror. Read it when you're stuck.

Let it become your light when things get dark.

Now it's time to celebrate. You've made it through the C: Clear Concept. That's a big deal. This is what you came for! Take the rest of the day off, eat a delish meal and come back refreshed and ready to move forward.

Part 2: From Idea to Action: Validating Your Vision

(5 minutes)

Now that your Clear Concept is alive and glowing, we shift into action mode.

I think of this part like a pair of scissors—we've opened wide to gather ideas, and now we close in to cut a clear path forward.

But before we move on, let's be honest with ourselves:
Is this the vision you're ready to build?

L: Legit & Long-Lasting: Vision Check-In

Before you invest your precious time, energy, and heart, let's make sure this Clear Vision is worthy of it.

Let's validate:
Is your Clear Vision 2 legit 2 quit? Is it meaningful and built to last?

Answer the following questions honestly:

- Am I called from head to toe to create my Clear Vision? Yes / No
- Does it need to be in the world, and am I the right person to do it? Yes / No
- Will I grow because I bring this vision to life? Yes / No
- Will I leave the world better by investing in this? Yes / No
- Will I stand up for this vision, come hell or high water? Yes / No
- Am I committed to navigating the highs and lows to make this real? Yes / No
- Is this the right time? Yes / No

If you answered "yes" to all of the questions, congrats! This vision is legit!

If not? That's valuable information. Head back to your Clear Concept brainstorming and revisit the parts that felt forced, flat, or uninspiring. Refine and return.

E: Expanded Energy: Becoming the Vessel for Your Vision

Clearly, you can't build something vibrant from a burned-out state.

Expanded Energy is what keeps you lit up when life gets messy.

It gives you the personal power to stay in the game, the radiance to attract aligned opportunities, and the groundedness to hear divine inspiration and trust it.

This isn't about "doing more." It's about becoming the version of yourself who can hold, lead, and live the vision you're creating.

You're the vessel. Let's power up.

Creating an Energetic Ecosystem

In my work, I've learned that if I want to write books, guide powerful client sessions, create content, give talks, and live in inspiration—not obligation—I need to treat my energy like sacred currency.

Here's what that looks like for me:

- I wake up at 6 a.m. to journal and listen to meditative music before the rest of the world gets noisy.
- I schedule hot yoga 3–4 times a week, yes, for fitness, but also the reset.
- I strengthen my root chakra regularly to feel safe in my body and my power.
- I set a bedtime (yes, like a toddler) because I know sleep = clarity.
- I curate my environment by surrounding myself with high-frequency people and minimizing small talk and low-vibe spaces.
- I hire support for my home and business so I can stay in my zone of genius

That's not a "morning routine;" that's a lifestyle built around honoring my energy so I can be the vessel for my Clear Vision to come to life.

What Is Expanded Energy?

Expanded Energy is how you embody your vision. Instead of thinking about it, you become it.

It doesn't come from green juice and to-do lists (though I'm not mad at either). It comes from rituals, movement, nourishment, boundaries, and soul-deep connection to your personal power.

In the next Bright Tools, you'll explore how to:

- Balance your chakras to ignite energy flow
- Perform the Magnetic Release Ritual to clear what's stuck
- Declare the future version of who you're becoming to match your Clear Vision

Mindset is the number one thing that separates you from your vision. Period. Put it on my tombstone. I know firsthand these rituals work for visionaries, creatives, and leaders who are 100 percent committed to building their future vision.

Let's begin.

THE C.L.E.A.R. VISION FRAMEWORK: BUILDING AND EMBODYING YOUR CLEAR VISION

Bright Tool: Balance Your Chakras

Let's talk about the highest level of energy that fuels your creativity, confidence, and connection to something bigger than you.

Chakras.

Chakras are ancient, wise, and incredibly effective inner power tools for anyone deeply rooted in purpose.

You've likely felt your chakras in action, even if you didn't have the language for it:

- That lump in your throat when you're afraid to speak up? That's your throat chakra.
- That pit in your stomach before a hard conversation? Hello, solar plexus.
- That tightness in your chest when you feel disconnected from someone you love? Yep, heart chakra territory.

Chakras are energy centers in your body. Think of them as your internal power grid, each one linked to different emotional, physical, and spiritual functions. When they're flowing freely, you feel grounded, lit up, and aligned. When they're blocked, you feel stuck, scattered, or off.

This is another layer to Pop and Drop Thinking, but laser-focused on self-awareness and alignment before the Drop.

As you move through each chakra center, ask yourself:

- Which chakra feels most activated right now?
- Which one feels blocked or off?
- What small action can I take to bring one chakra back into balance this week?

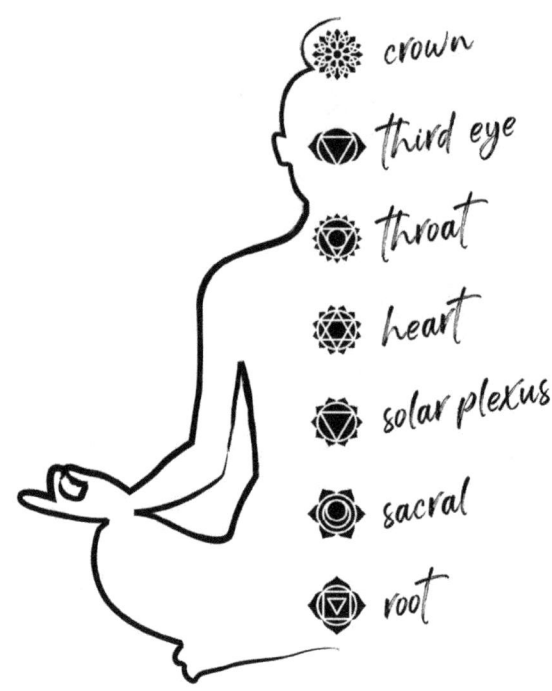

Root Chakra

Location: Base of your spine
Theme: Safety, stability, identity
Imbalance Signs: Anxiety, fear, lack of direction
Pop Energy Practice: Hip-opening yoga, grounding breath

Ask Yourself:

- Do I feel grounded in my life right now? If not, why?

THE C.L.E.A.R. VISION FRAMEWORK: BUILDING AND EMBODYING YOUR CLEAR VISION

- Where do I need more structure or support?

- What helps me feel safe in my body?

Mantras:

- I am safe, grounded, and supported.
- I trust myself and my path.
- My vision is rooted in truth.

Sacral Chakra

Location: Below the navel
Theme: Creativity, flow, pleasure
Imbalance Signs: Burnout, repression, creative blocks
Pop Energy Practice: Dance, bath, time in water

Ask Yourself:

- Where am I denying myself joy or pleasure?

- What does creativity mean to me?

- How can I bring more play into my work?

Mantras:

- My creativity is sacred.

THE C.L.E.A.R. VISION FRAMEWORK: BUILDING AND EMBODYING YOUR CLEAR VISION

- I am allowed to enjoy life.
- I trust the flow of my emotions.

Solar Plexus Chakra

Location: Upper abdomen
Theme: Confidence, willpower, self-trust
Imbalance Signs: Self-doubt, people-pleasing, indecision
Pop Energy Practice: Power poses, core work, priming breathwork

Ask Yourself:

- Where am I holding back my power?

- What decision am I afraid to make?

- What would I do today if I fully trusted myself?

Mantras:

- I am capable and courageous.
- I follow my intuition with confidence.
- I am a powerful creator.

Heart Chakra

Location: Center of the chest
Theme: Love, connection, compassion
Imbalance Signs: Walls up, resentment, loneliness
Pop Energy Practice: Hand-to-heart breathing

Ask Yourself:

- What am I holding onto that I need to release?

THE C.L.E.A.R. VISION FRAMEWORK: BUILDING AND EMBODYING YOUR CLEAR VISION

- Where can I offer more love to myself?

  [ ]

- What makes my heart feel soft and open?

  [ ]

Mantras:

- I radiate and receive love freely.
- I am worthy of love.
- I love myself.

Throat Chakra

Location: Throat
Theme: Expression, truth, boundaries
Imbalance Signs: Holding back, fear of judgment, over-explaining
Pop Energy Practice: Say your Clear Vision aloud

Ask Yourself:

- Where am I not speaking up when I want to?

- What needs to be said, even if it's uncomfortable?

- What would it feel like to be fully heard?

Mantras:

- My voice matters.
- I express myself clearly and confidently.
- I am safe to speak my truth.

Third Eye Chakra

Location: Between the eyebrows
Theme: Intuition, vision, insight
Imbalance Signs: Overthinking, confusion, disconnection
Pop Energy Practice: Silent meditation, visualization of your Clear Vision realized

Ask Yourself:

- Am I listening to my intuition or overriding it?

- What would change if I trusted myself?

- What am I being guided toward right now?

Mantras:

- I trust my inner wisdom.
- I see clearly.
- My intuition leads the way.

Crown Chakra

Location: Top of the head
Theme: Purpose, spirituality, higher self
Imbalance Signs: Cynicism, lack of inspiration, disconnection
Pop Energy Practice: Visualize a lotus blooming at your crown

Ask Yourself:

- Why am I here, on earth, right now?

THE C.L.E.A.R. VISION FRAMEWORK: BUILDING AND EMBODYING YOUR CLEAR VISION

- When do I feel most connected to spirit, source, or flow?

- What area of my life do I need to accept and surrender to?

Mantras:

- I am connected to something greater.
- I trust the unfolding of my life.
  I am always supported.

> **Bright Tip:**
> Choose one chakra to focus on this week. Pick a mantra and a Pop Practice. Set a phone reminder to anchor it into your day.

Do not skip this step.

Bright Tool: The Magnetic Release Ritual

The Magnetic Release Ritual is a powerful somatic practice designed to clear energetic clutter—those Drop Thoughts, patterns of self-doubt, and sticky energy that block your clarity and weigh you down.

When you release what no longer serves you, you create space for clarity, alignment, and the freedom to create something new.

How to Perform the Magnetic Release Ritual

1. Ground & Set Your Space
Sit comfortably on the floor, cross-legged or whatever feels grounded. Keep your spine tall and your body relaxed. Optional: light a candle or incense to signal intentional clearing.

2. Position Your Hands
Place your left hand, palm up, on your knee, open to receive energy.
Raise your right hand slightly in front of your body, facing you, like a magnet that is ready to scan and "pull" Drop energy out.

3. Begin at the Root
Slowly circle your right hand near your lower pelvis, just in front of your root chakra. Notice what sensations or heat arise. You don't need to analyze, just observe.

4. Move Up the Body
Gently move your hand up the front of your body, stopping at each of the six chakra points:

- Sacral (just below the navel)
- Solar Plexus (stomach)
- Heart (center chest)
- Throat
- Third Eye (between your brows)
- Crown (top of your head)

THE C.L.E.A.R. VISION FRAMEWORK: BUILDING AND EMBODYING YOUR CLEAR VISION

At each point, pause and feel for heat, heaviness, tightness, or stuck energy. Visualize your hand drawing that energy out and sticking to the magnet.

5. Release It All
Once you reach your crown chakra at the top, sweep your hand upward and away from your body. Imagine throwing that energy into the light, the earth, or the wind, whatever imagery feels most powerful to you.

Say (silently or aloud):
"I release what no longer serves me and am making space for new energy."

Finally, take a few deep breaths and repeat the ritual as needed, especially after intense conversations, stressful events, or when you feel misaligned or heavy.

Do not skip this step.

Journal Prompt:

- What part of your body held the most tension?

- What emotion, memory, or belief might be tied to that area?

- What would it feel like to be free of it for good?

THE C.L.E.A.R. VISION FRAMEWORK: BUILDING AND EMBODYING YOUR CLEAR VISION

Bright Tool: Are You a Hell Yes? Or A Hell No? Consult your Visionary Values.

You've done the deep work to explore your energy, align your chakras, and release what no longer serves you. Now, it's time to declare what you are a Hell Yes and a Hell No for.

When your energy is aligned and your values are locked in, decision-making gets easier.

You don't spiral. You don't over-explain.

You just know.

You know what's right for you because it either matches your energy or it doesn't. It's either a Hell Yes or a Hell No.

Your Visionary Values act as a simple filter to assess choices and opportunities through the lens of your future self. They guide how you show up, what you stand for, and what you want to be known for. When clearly defined, they make decisions a whole lot easier—saving you time and energy.

Unlike traditional corporate values (trust, innovation, integrity, snooze), your Visionary Values are deeply personal. They reflect your style, beliefs, creative flair, quirks, and leadership edge.

If your name came up and you weren't in the room, what do you want them to say about you?

"Oh, Ruby? She's someone who believes in..."

Let's find out what fills in the blank.

The Dinner Party Exercise

This tool is adapted from the original Visionary Values practice in *Find Your Clear Vision* and has evolved through years of coaching creative leaders and visionaries like you.

Step 1: Who Inspires You?

Imagine hosting a dinner party and inviting four to six people—alive or dead, real or fictional—who inspire you. These are individuals whose ideas, style, presence, intelligence, or creativity you deeply admire.

Don't overthink it. There are no wrong answers here.

Ask yourself:

- Who do I admire or look up to?
- Whose posts do I always like on social?
- Who do I look up to?
- Whose books do I read front to back?
- Who would I want to be mentored by or have a glass of wine with?

Here are mine:
Elton John, Gwyneth Paltrow, Emma Stone, Madonna, Amy Porterfield, Beyoncé, and Michelle Obama.

These people are performers, ridiculously creative visionaries, and powerful business owners. They speak my language, and I know what they stand for.

THE C.L.E.A.R. VISION FRAMEWORK: BUILDING AND EMBODYING YOUR CLEAR VISION

Write yours down.

Step 2: Why Do They Inspire You?

Next, explore why these people light you up.

- What are they known *for*?
- What values do they live out loud?
- What do they believe in, speak about, or unapologetically embody?
- What about their approach to life or work speaks to your soul?

For example, if you love Broadway performers but can't sing or dance—that's not the point. You might be drawn to their boldness, discipline, emotional expression, or ability to take up space.

Those are the deeper values to look for in your people.

Try to uncover 3-4 words or ideas that capture what each person represents to you.

Step 3: Highlight the Patterns

Now, look for themes. What words, qualities, or values show up again and again? Highlight them.

Because guess what? What you admire in them is a mirror of what you most value.

This is the beginning of your Visionary Value Venn Diagram: three core values that represent what matters most to you, stripped of the surface layer of what you *think* you should value.

Mine?
Fun
Creative
Business

I run a fun, creative business. Of course, I do. These values shape the rooms I want to be in and the conversations I want to lead.

And yours will too, because they are unique to you.

Why This Matters

Your Visionary Values help you make decisions from a place of clarity; you know what you like and can see what falls outside of those boundaries.

Test it out. When presented with an opportunity, ask yourself: Is this aligned with my Visionary Values?

If you're a Hell Yes, the answer is clear.

If it aligns with only one, then Hell No. If it aligns with two, you have to make the call. Ask yourself: Is this moving me towards or away from my Clear Vision? Choose accordingly.

BUILD YOUR CLEAR VISION

Visionary Values

THE C.L.E.A.R. VISION FRAMEWORK: BUILDING AND EMBODYING YOUR CLEAR VISION

Part 3: Creating Your Success Path

Aspirational Success + Rooted in Celebration

You've envisioned it. Declared it. Aligned your energy.

Now, let's turn your vision into reality.

This phase of the C.L.E.A.R. Vision Framework is all about momentum—taking the brilliance of your Clear Concept and giving it structure, movement, and forward progress. This is where your inner vision becomes an external reality. And we do it all in a way that feels energizing, aligned, and sustainable.

In the following sections, you'll map your success path and anchor it with celebration. Because yes, structure matters, but so do joy, fun, and celebration.

A: Aspirational Success: Bringing Your Vision to Life

This is the phase where you shift from imagining to embodying.

Some Clear Visions are big—like launching a non-profit to end loneliness, creating a support group for parents and kids with ADHD, building a coaching practice from scratch, writing a book, or transforming your lifestyle.

Others are quieter but just as powerful: creating more space for joy, developing consistency in your creative work, or saying yes to your intuition more often.

No matter the scope, all Clear Visions begin with one thing: intentional action.

Choose Your Path: Sprint or Track?

Not all visions require the same level of time, energy, or structure. Some are ready for a sprint. Others call for a marathon mindset.

The 90-Day Clear Vision Sprint
For focused, short-term breakthroughs that build energy and confidence. Ideal for:

- Learning how to teach yoga
- Learning a new language
- Upleveling your lifestyle or diet
- Finding your next role
- Launching a smaller project (like a podcast or website)
- Exploring a creative or spiritual practice

The 12-Month Vision Track
I know from experience that the bigger the vision, the longer it takes to create.

My client Cathi came back to work with me a year after her vision came to life: becoming the CEO of her family business, selling her home, and renovating an old shoe warehouse into a live-work space.

My client Jess, who moved to Puerto Rico and built a coaching practice based on the work of Abraham-Hicks, recently DM'd me to say, "Everything we talked about a year ago came true."

My first book, *Find Your Clear Vision*, started with the idea, "Wouldn't it be cool to write this book?" Two years later, it was in my hands.

The 12-month Vision Track is ideal for:

- Writing a book
- Starting a non-profit
- Implementing a new business model
- Building what's next after traditional "retirement"
- Building a new brand or business
- Transitioning into a new identity or leadership role

THE C.L.E.A.R. VISION FRAMEWORK: BUILDING AND EMBODYING YOUR CLEAR VISION

Ask yourself: What phase of the journey am I in? Do I need quick momentum, or am I ready for intentional expansion?

Success Visualization

Let's begin by feeling into what success looks and feels like for you. Ask yourself these questions, or simply close your eyes and imagine your vision coming to life.

- What do you see happening around you?

THE C.L.E.A.R. VISION FRAMEWORK: BUILDING AND EMBODYING YOUR CLEAR VISION

- What have you created?

- Who is impacted by your vision?

THE C.L.E.A.R. VISION FRAMEWORK: BUILDING AND EMBODYING YOUR CLEAR VISION

- Who are you serving, and how is that brought to life?

- What changes do we see you making in your life?

THE C.L.E.A.R. VISION FRAMEWORK: BUILDING AND EMBODYING YOUR CLEAR VISION

- How does it feel in your body?

- What unexpected joy has emerged because your vision has become a reality?

Now complete these declarations:

In (90 days or 12 months):

- I have created:

- I have launched:

THE C.L.E.A.R. VISION FRAMEWORK: BUILDING AND EMBODYING YOUR CLEAR VISION

- I have manifested:

These statements create energetic clarity. They tell the universe: *I'm serious, and I'm ready, let's go.*

> **Bright Tip:**
> When I was building my practice, I used this process weekly. Every Monday morning, I'd sit down, light a candle, and re-read my vision declarations like a prayer. It reminded me why I started, especially on the hard days. I even taped one to my mirror. Not because I needed a motivational quote but because I needed a reminder of where I was going.

Reality Bridge (AI Prompt)

Now comes the fun part: what does a "day in the life" of your visionary self look like, the one who's actively bringing your vision to life?

Let's ask AI.

(P.S. AI moves fast—probably even faster than when I published this book. For the most up-to-date AI prompts I'm using with my clients, pop over to bebrightlisa.com/books.)

Use this prompt to illuminate your path:

AI Prompt:
Based on my future vision (insert your Clear Vision declaration and Success declaration and any details AI needs to know to understand and "see" your vision), help me:

- *Identify daily actions that will make this vision real*
- *Recommend books, podcasts, or resources aligned with my vision*
- *Name possible challenges I may face*
- *Define the support I'll need, personal and professional*
- *Create or refine the systems that will help me stay aligned with my vision*

Here's another AI Prompt:
Let's pretend my Clear Vision is a book with each month of the year being a chapter in the book that creates my Clear Vision. Please:

- *Suggest 3 potential titles for my Clear Vision*
- *Create monthly chapter titles for the year (we're currently in [insert month])*
- *For each month/chapter, include:*
  - *A title for the month/chapter*
  - *The main focus*
  - *Key milestones*
  - *Specific action steps*
  - *A success marker or moment to create by the end of the month*

THE C.L.E.A.R. VISION FRAMEWORK: BUILDING AND EMBODYING YOUR CLEAR VISION

Optional: Use your favorite energetic words, your Word of the Year, metaphors, movies, or books as themes.

For example, one year, my Word of the Year was *Glow*.
So January's title was "Ignite the Spark," and February was "Illuminating Vision."

Don't get caught in the web of details. This isn't about "doing it all"—god no. It's about honoring your vision with structure.

Structure is what brings your creative flow to life.

The 90-Day Clear Vision Sprint Map

Here's how your 90-day sprint can flow. Brainstorm the answers for these three key phases. You can do it on your own, or pop it into AI for extra support and ideas.

Month 1: Foundation Building

- What three elements of your vision need immediate attention? And when will they be completed?

- What support systems will you put in place?

- What daily practices will you establish?

THE C.L.E.A.R. VISION FRAMEWORK: BUILDING AND EMBODYING YOUR CLEAR VISION

- What does the beginning, middle and end of your vision journey look like? Name the big milestones.

Month 2: Growth and Development

- What skills do you need to develop? By when?

- What connections do you need to make? By when?

- What's the next step to complete the middle milestone?

Month 3: Implementation and Review

- What tangible results do you want to see?

- How will you measure progress?

THE C.L.E.A.R. VISION FRAMEWORK: BUILDING AND EMBODYING YOUR CLEAR VISION

- What adjustments are needed?

- What's outstanding? What are the next steps?

Boom.

There's your map. Beginning, middle and end.

Now grab your map and hit the road.

After 90 days, when you are living your dream, review, refine and keep going.

Weekly Energetic Rituals to Uplevel Your Intentional Action

Clear action must be paired with clear energy, or we lose sight of the big vision.

These three rituals are simple but powerful to weave into your day.

On Mondays:

- Clear with the Magnetic Release Ritual
- Re-read your Clear Vision declaration
- Journal on what feels most alive
- Choose one focus for the week ahead

Create a Weekly Sacred Hour:

- Block 30–60 minutes per day for your vision
- Use it for action, creativity, connection, and whatever fuels your next step
- This is a sacred, non-negotiable time
  (*Example: I schedule my Sacred Hour from 6–7 a.m. before the house wakes up. I meditate, visualize, and journal.*)

Friday Reflection

- What worked this week?

THE C.L.E.A.R. VISION FRAMEWORK: BUILDING AND EMBODYING YOUR CLEAR VISION

- What did I learn?

- What needs to shift next week?

One client used her Friday Reflections to track wins, big and small. When she felt stuck mid-month, she'd re-read her list and realize how far she'd come.

These rituals are how you stay in a relationship with your future self.
Trust her. She's waiting for you at the end of your vision.

Part 4: Rooted in Celebration:

Staying Nourished on the Journey

Celebration is one of my core values. I simply call it *fun*.
Not party-hat fun. I'm talking grounded, soul-expanding, real-freaking-life joy.

This is where you honor what you've done and who you're becoming.
Not just when you've "made it" but throughout the journey.

When one of my clients launched her group coaching program, she booked a solo weekend getaway. No balloons. No big party. Just time to savor what she'd created.

Another bought herself peonies every Friday because her visionary self loves beauty.

These moments matter.

Celebration rewires your brain to associate growth with joy, not just grind. It sustains motivation, creates emotional safety, and helps you embody your Clear Vision with more ease and delight.

Hard work is a tool. But so is play, rest, and fun.

Your Celebration Menu

Use this menu to design your Bright Celebrations. Go back to your Creative Identity and all the fun and imaginative things you dreamed up, and add them here.

Big Milestone Celebrations:

- Book a weekend getaway
- Take private dance or voice lessons
- Splurge on that jacket or sequined dress that feels like your future self

THE C.L.E.A.R. VISION FRAMEWORK: BUILDING AND EMBODYING YOUR CLEAR VISION

Progress Celebrations (Monthly/Weekly Wins)

- Schedule a massage
- Try a new creative activity (flower pressing, pottery, improv)
- Take your kids somewhere fun just to play. When was the last time you were on a swing??
- Sleep in

Daily Victories

- Turn on your Pop Playlist (you can find mine on Spotify)
- Ring a celebration bell
- Text a friend your "win of the day"

Create a Personal Celebration Menu

Big Milestone Celebrations:

1.
2.
3.

In-Progress Celebrations:

1.
2.
3.

Daily Victories:

1.
2.
3.

Choose one and schedule it now. Yes, now. Open your calendar. Make it real.

Final Reflection: Your Vision in Motion

Success isn't just about doing more; it's about aligning your energy, intentions, and actions so your Clear Vision becomes reality.

With your Energetic Rituals, Visionary Values, Timelines, and Celebration Menu, you now have a full ecosystem to bring your future into the present.

But this isn't the end; it's the beginning.

What you've created here is a foundation for conscious transformation.
A living, breathing framework that grows with you.
The next step? Choosing to return to it again and again.

This is your Clear Vision in motion.

Chapter 4:

YOUR CLEAR VISION RISING

Friend, take a breath with me.
In.
And out.

Feel the shift that's already happened within you. You're not the same person who began this journey. You've awakened to your power as a visionary—blending energetic wisdom with modern technology, practical strategy with spiritual alignment.

Throughout this process, you've discovered that your Clear Vision isn't a fuzzy dream. It's a living force waiting to be expressed through you. The world needs your vision now more than ever.

In a volatile and ever-changing world, visionaries like you become lighthouses, yep, those shiny disco balls of light, showing what's possible when we dare to dream bigger and act on it.

Your vision is not just about personal transformation.

It's about contributing to the collective consciousness through your unique gifts, experiences, and perspective. You are here to build something meaningful—not just for yourself, but for those you're here to serve.

Right now, you hold a complete manual for turning vision into reality.
No more wondering how or when. You have the tools, clarity, and strategy to move forward with purpose and confidence.

Remember, this journey isn't meant to be walked alone.

As your visionary coach and guide, I'm here to support you as you bring your Clear Vision to life—whether you need to refresh your strategy, align your energy, or simply be reminded of your power.

Keep the Momentum

If this workbook lit a spark, imagine what we could create together in a full coaching journey.

Whether you're looking for private coaching, community support, or want to bring this work into your business or brand, I'm here to walk with you.

Visit www.bebrightlisa.com to learn more about how we can collaborate or gather a group of like-hearted friends and turn this workbook into a book club or creative circle.

Everything is better with an aligned community.

The time for hesitation is over. Your Clear Vision is calling, and you're ready to answer.

Your future self is watching, smiling, jumping for joy—knowing this is the moment everything changed.

Rise, Clear Visionary.

Your time is now.

Be bright,
Lisa

ACKNOWLEDGMENTS

Let's be real—no one builds a Clear Vision alone. This book wouldn't exist without my people.

Family—my ride or die:
Randy, Sam, Ben, Julien, and Catalina, I'm so grateful to do this wild, precious life with you. Thanks for the laughs, hugs, and endless inspiration.

Mom and Dad:
Dad, thanks for instilling in me a love of stories and tradition. Mom, thank you for joy, creativity, and always encouraging my wildest dreams. Your belief in me is why I believe in myself.

Lewis and Katie:
You show me what it means to live with integrity and love. Proud to be your sister.

To my disco-dancing, "hell yes" friends:
You make life big, bold, and bright. Thank you for cheering me on, showing up, and saying "Absolutely, let's do it!" to every crazy idea.

To my coaches, teachers, and all the magical humans who have held space for my growth:
Thank you for listening, nudging, and reminding me to keep going (even when it felt impossible).

To my clients—my visionaries:
You trust me with your stories and let me witness your transformation. This book is for you. You teach me as much as I guide you.

To everyone who pitched in on this book:
Your feedback, insights, and good vibes made all the difference. Thank you for helping me see this vision through.

And to the bright light that connects us all—thank you.

Be bright, Lisa

ABOUT THE AUTHOR

Lisa Guillot (Ghee-O) is a visionary brand and business coach, transformational leadership expert, and best-selling author. She guides visionaries, creatives, and leaders who are ready to move beyond traditional success and create what truly matters.

With over 20 years of experience in brand strategy and transformational coaching, Lisa's C.L.E.A.R. Vision Framework has helped hundreds of clients unlock their next chapter, expand their energy, and build meaningful businesses, projects, and lives with clarity and soul.

Lisa's approach is rooted in both strategy and spirit. She weaves together practical business insights with mindset work and energetic rituals, helping her clients align their inner world with outer action—so their vision is not just imagined, but fully embodied and expressed.

She works with executives, entrepreneurs, and thought leaders who are ready to move from overthinking to bold action—whether launching a new venture, developing intellectual property, or becoming a catalyst for change in their community.

Lisa is the author of *Find Your Clear Vision: A New Mindset to Create a Vibrant Personal or Professional Brand with Purpose* and host of the *Your Bright Personal Brand* podcast.

Connect with Lisa
Learn more, discover resources, or connect for coaching at bebrightlisa.com or on Instagram @bebrightlisa.

SPREAD THE WORD!

Loved this workbook? Do me a favor and:

- **Drop a Review:**
  Tell the world what you loved on Amazon, Goodreads, or wherever you hang out online.
- **Snap & Share:**
  Post a photo, tag @bebrightlisa, and show off your journey!
- **Gather Your Crew:**
  Start a book club, share with a friend, or just shout it from the rooftops. We create more magic when we do it together.

Thank you for being part of the Clear Vision movement. Now—let's light up the world.

www.ingramcontent.com/pod-product-compliance
Lightning Source LLC
Chambersburg PA
CBHW060506240426
43661CB00007B/932